MOTORCYCLING

MOTORCYCLING

======= **CHARLES COOMBS**

illustrated with 26 photographs
William Morrow and Company
New York

Published simultaneously in Canada by
George J. McLeod Limited, Toronto.

Printed in the United States of America.

Library of Congress Catalog Card Number 68–23911.

8   9   10   75   74   73

Acknowledgments for Photographs

American Honda Motor Company, 23, 72
Automobile Club of Southern California, 47
Charles Coombs, FRONTISPIECE, 19, 26, 27, 39, 67
Croft Manufacturing Company, 68
Harley-Davidson Motor Company, 11
Los Angeles Police Department, 76, 77
Motorcycle, Scooter & Allied Trades Association, 54, 61
The Triumph Corporation, 82, 87, 91, 93
Yamaha International Corporation, 15, 25, 35, 51, 65, 71

CONTENTS

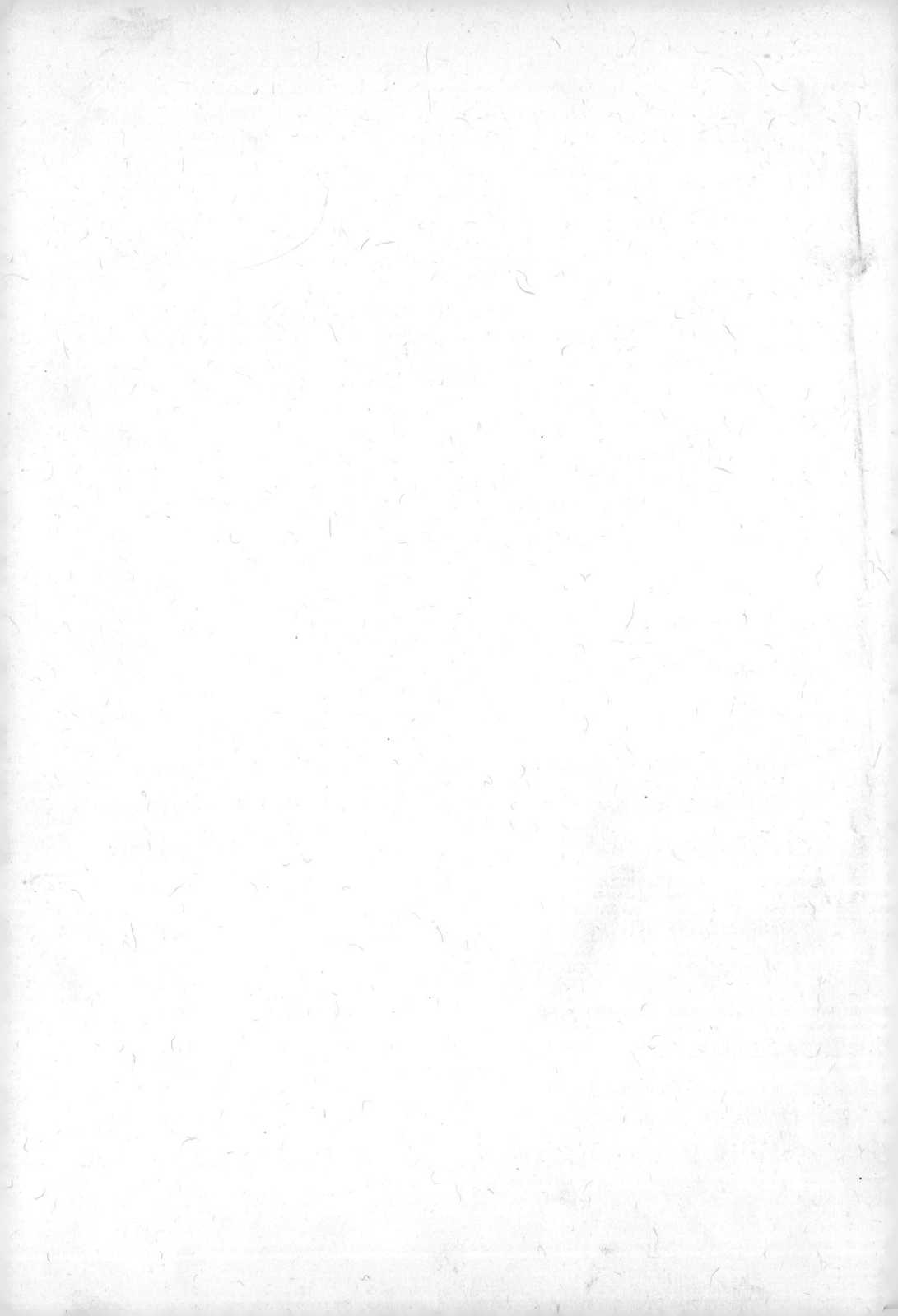

THE WORLD OF TWO-WHEELERS

Vrooom—VROOOM!

Across the nation, day and night, young people flip switches, kick starter pedals, and twist hand throttles feeding fuel into the hungry cylinder heads of their motorbikes.

Vrooom—VROOOM!

That sound has been heard on the American scene for generations, and it promises to continue and even to increase as rapidly growing numbers of young people explore the fun, adventure, economy, and practicality of riding two-wheeled motorized vehicles.

Generally speaking, motorcycles and motor scooters are a twentieth-century development, although numerous experiments with power-driven

9

two-wheelers were carried on at earlier dates. Small, lightweight, high-powered gasoline engines were difficult to build, so the motorcycle industry was slow to develop. During World War I American cycle manufacturing gained impetus when the United States Army bought thousands of motorcycles to be used by dispatch riders, ammunition carriers, medical corpsmen, and even machine-gun teams on the Western Front. Indian and Harley-Davidson models, some with and some without sidecars, were purchased by the Army.

Since motorcycles remained expensive following the war, they were used largely by prosperous hobbyists, thrill-seeking daredevils, and law enforcement officers. The cycles of this period were noisy, uncomfortable, and usually unreliable.

During the Second World War motorcycles again were put to good use in troop convoys, courier service, and military police work. By the end of the war motorcycles had developed into powerful, efficient machines. They were still fairly heavy and expensive to purchase, although

10

cheap to operate. The cycles were used primarily as low-cost transportation and for work assignments; sport and pleasure riding remained occasional activities of the owners. The powered two-wheelers were still at this time an unusual sight on public streets and highways.

Only within the last decade or so have lightweight, inexpensive motorbikes become readily available to provide the fun and utility of two-wheeled, engine-driven transportation for many people. Now it has become both fashionable and practical to use a motorcycle or a motor scooter

Lightweight machines are favorite runabouts for most of today's cyclists.

for business as well as pleasure. Doctors, lawyers, bankers, teachers, actors, secretaries—all are discovering the advantages of having a lightweight motorbike in their garage, ready to go at a moment's notice. There are many reasons for this growing popularity of motorcycling.

In most parts of the world, motorcycles have become an economic necessity because of the low-cost transportation they provide. When visiting any foreign country—Latin American, European, Oriental, or African—one immediately becomes aware of the large number of two-wheeled motor vehicles on city streets and rural roads. Motorbikes—both cycles and scooters—often far outnumber automobiles, which are much more costly to buy, maintain, and operate.

In the United States, where many people own cars, motorcycling has always been more of a novelty than a necessity. Yet more and more cycles are being used all the time. One reason for this increasing use is urban congestion. Cities, and the highways connecting them, are seriously overcrowded with cars, and a motorbike can be

12

maneuvered to avoid most of this traffic. With his lunch pail strapped to the rear rack, a factory or office worker can cycle to work with relative ease, weaving through the jungle of bumper-to-bumper automobiles. Not only does he enjoy the invigorating freshness of the wind in his face, he avoids those aggravating parking problems which most city motorists face. Furthermore, he may get a hundred or more miles to a single gallon of gas.

The lightweight motorcycle, which became so popular that it revolutionized the entire industry, was first built by the Japanese firm of Honda. The style was quickly taken up by many other manufacturers.

Soichiro Honda is the son of a Japanese blacksmith. His fascination with machines began when he was a child of four or five living in a small village near the city of Hamamatsu, Japan. An average student in school, Honda particularly enjoyed his science and mathematics courses. He was a middle-aged man, a specialist in metallurgy and mechanics, when Japan plunged into World War II in 1941. By the time the war ended, in

13

1945, he was running a small factory that made piston rings for Japanese war machines.

After the war, while casting around for something to do, Mr. Honda picked up cheaply 500 small, war-surplus gas engines, which had been used to power communications equipment. He adapted them so they could be fitted to bicycles to provide the needed motive power and relieve the cyclist of having to use the muscle power of his legs. After his stock of war-surplus engines was gone, Honda began manufacturing his own engines. The next step, logically, was to manufacture the lightweight motorcycle frames, the wheels, the whole works needed to go with the small engines.

The first of these foreign-made machines arrived in the United States around 1960. Demand for the lightweight cycles became so great that Honda Motor Company quickly expanded into a massive manufacturing enterprise—today the world's largest maker of motorcycles.

The handy two-wheelers, selling for less than $300 and getting up to 200 miles per gallon of gas, became the hallmark of the young generation. Although the name Honda became almost synonymous with lightweight sport motorcycling, such other Japanese firms as Yamaha, Suzuki, Kawasaki, and Hodaka began to offer similar well-engineered, lightweight machines throughout the world. Long familiar to American cyclists, England's famed BSA, Triumph, and Norton motorbikes, of different weights and power

Motorized two-wheelers are growing more popular every day.

now are imported in ever-increasing numbers. Spain, Italy, and Germany, where motorbikes have been widespread for many years, also have high-quality machines on the United States market.

With the sudden new boom in cycling, Harley-Davidson, the old and reputable American firm, increased its domestic output of middleweight and heavy machines, and also put a lightweight model on the market. However, the company is still known primarily for the production of the so-called "big lungers"—the heavier two-cylinder bikes used by touring riders, policemen, and the armed forces.

Thus, the sales and use of the motorized two-wheelers have continued to increase steadily. From a total number of about 500,000 cycles registered in 1960, the quantity skyrocketed to well over two million by the end of 1967. Today motorbike manufacturers and dealers are looking toward sales of a million machines a year.

There is little doubt that the two-wheelers are here to stay.

16

NUTS AND BOLTS

The world of motorbikes is vast and varied. Starting with the pocket-sized minibikes, usually powered by small lawnmower-type motors, it encompasses motor scooters, lightweight street bikes, sport cycles, and big two-wheeled machines, having perhaps fifty or so horsepower . . . enough to make them fly if wings were added!

There are dozens of motorcycle manufacturers, large and small, and scores of different cycle models. Some machines are tailored to fit special uses. However, most basic motorcycles are made to suit a variety of riding activities.

The most popular machines are the lightweights. They use small one- and two-cylinder engines of between five and thirty horsepower, an

17

ample amount to get them around town or out into the country. Some lightweight machines are too slow or too low-powered to be allowed on high-speed turnpikes or freeways. They are, however, perfectly suited to normal use on city streets and for general running around town, going to school, or exploring back-country dirt trails.

After the lightweights come the middleweight and heavyweight motorcycles. These larger machines are a little more specialized. For instance, a drag-racing motorcycle or one groomed for breaking speed records on an oval track or on the smooth straightaways of Utah's Bonneville salt flats isn't much good for neighborhood riding. A big touring cycle, complete with buddy seat, windscreen, and hand-carved saddlebags—or panniers—is relatively useless for rugged hill climbs. But despite differences in size, power, and cost, motorcycles are designed and built primarily to be straddled by one or two persons going from one place to another, and all cycles have certain features in common.

The core of any motorcycle is its engine. Since

the machine is small, the engine is comparatively compact and simple. Most motorcycle engines are designed around one or two cylinders. Some are of the valveless two-stroke variety in which the cylinder head fires with each revolution of the piston. Or they may be four-stroke, or four-cycle, power plants, complete with valves and rods. In the four-cycle engine the cylinder fires on every other revolution of the piston. Both engines have certain advantages.

A thirty-horsepower, two-cylinder, four-stroke
engine is typical for middleweight motorcycles.

The four-stroke engine has more working parts than the two-stroke and performs smoothly over a wide range of operations. It idles well, runs steadily at slow speeds, and is even more efficient during high-speed operation. Since the cylinder fires only on every second piston stroke, there is an extra cooling period between sparks, which makes the four-cycle engine less prone to over-heating than the two-cycle type. Virtually all automobile engines are of the four-stroke design.

The two-stroke power plant, having fewer moving parts, is less susceptible to breakdowns and is simpler to maintain. The four-cycle engine must have a separate oil tank and pump to feed the lubricant into it. The two-cycle engine simply mixes the oil with the gasoline and sprays it into the engine as a single solution that provides for both combustion and lubrication.

Motorcyclists are forever locked in disputes about the pros and cons of two-stroke versus four-stroke power plants. There are no pat answers to the argument. Both engines perform steadily and sturdily. The more simple two-

20

stroke type seems best suited to the lightweight and middleweight machines, while the four-strokers are generally preferred in the heavier engines of over 250cc displacement. (The traditional method of rating engine size is by cubic centimeters [cc's] of displacement—the total volume of space swept by the pistons of all the cylinders during one complete stroke of each piston.)

During operation of the motorcycle, the engine, through the gears of the transmission, turns the front chain sprocket. A few cycles are driven by shafts geared directly to the motor, a design similar to that of an automobile, but most motorcycles are chain powered. From the front, or power, sprocket the chain loops over the toothed disc of the rear sprocket on the back wheel, furnishing drive. The sprocket sizes depend largely upon the purpose for which the machine is intended. The larger the rear sprocket, the slower the cycle, but the better its ability to climb hills or prowl along dirt trails. As in an automobile the speed and pulling power can be varied by shifting gears in the transmission. Most motor-cycles have at least four forward speeds, but no reverse.

With a gas tank to furnish fuel to the carbure-tor, and a muffler to soften the bark of the high-speed engine, the motive power is complete.

The engine controls are made up of a clutch lever mounted on the left handlebar and a twist throttle built into the grip on the right handlebar. The gearshift pedal on virtually all modern mo-torcycles is worked by one foot. It can be on either side of the machine. The British cycles favor the pedal on the right side, while German and Japanese manufacturers locate theirs on the left. Other makes vary the position.

Regardless of the side on which the shift pedal is located, the rear-brake pedal will be near the rider's foot on the opposite side. The front brake is operated by a hand lever located on the right handlebar near the throttle grip.

Opposite: The parts of a motorcycle, as shown in these side views are basically the same on all machines.

CLUTCH LEVER · THROTTLE GRIP · GAS TANK · DUAL SADDLE · INSTRUMENTS · IGNITION SWITCH · FRONT BRAKE · FOOT PEG · GEARSHIFT PEDAL · TRANSMISSION · CENTER STAND · REAR FOOT PEG · CHAIN SPROCKET

HORN AND LIGHT DIMMER BUTTONS (AT BASE OF LEFT-HAND GRIP) · THROTTLE · FRONT-BRAKE LEVER · GAS PETCOCK · CARBURETOR · AIR CLEANER · AR SHOCK ABSORBERS · MOTOR · FOOT PEG · REAR-BRAKE PEDAL · MUFFLER · KICK STARTER

Naturally, before mounting any machine, the rider must make sure which side has the gearshift pedal and which the brake. He must also have the presence of mind to adapt to each cycle and be able to overcome habits developed while operating vehicles that may have had the controls on opposite sides. On a few motorcycles the rear brake and gearshift pedals can be put on whichever sides are preferred by the rider.

Some motorcycles shift into first, or low, gear by pushing the gear-shift pedal down past the neutral notch, then into second, third, and fourth gears by lifting, or "toeing," the pedal up. Other cycles reverse the pattern and are shifted into low by lifting up on the pedal, then pushing down through neutral into second, third, and fourth gears. This difference is but another reason why a new rider should check out a cycle carefully before starting it up.

Although the engine and brakes are the essential parts that start and stop the motorcycle, a proper machine possesses many other items of equipment for the comfort and safety of riders.

24

Here a rider is "toeing" a gearshift pedal up.

Fenders repel mud and water. A chain guard performs the important function of preventing the chain from fouling or throwing mud or grease on the rider. The cycle, if it is to be used on streets or highways, is required by law to have approved lights, both front and rear. The front light should have both upper and lower beams. The red taillight must be bright enough for easy visibility and have a white downward beam to illuminate the license plate.

Often the engine and riding instruments are

located in the headlight housing, or they can be mounted on the handlebars or gas tank. These instruments normally include a speedometer and a tachometer to indicate engine revolutions per minute (rpm's). In addition, there may be several small warning lights to give the rider such information as whether the ignition switch is on or off (to prevent loss of battery power), whether the transmission is in neutral before kicking the

Riding instruments and hand controls
are within easy view and reach.

starter, and if the headlight is on high beam. Different motorcycles may have additional instruments, but those mentioned are the basic ones.

For smooth riding the motorcycle must have good springs and shock absorbers at both front and rear. The better types of springs and shocks are easily adjustable. There is nothing more aggravating, tiring, or, in fact, risky than springs or shock absorbers that are too stiff or too soft.

This rear view of a lightweight bike shows shock absorbers, sprocket, chain guard, and street-type tire.

Comfort also depends largely upon the seat or saddle with which the cycle is equipped. The dual seat is by far the most popular with the normal street-touring motorcyclist. Not only does it provide room for a passenger, but it allows the single rider to change position now and then, avoiding soreness and fatigue. Although leather still is used on some seats, most are covered by one of many plastic fabrics and vinyl materials. A dual saddle or buddy seat should have some kind of a strap or handhold for the passenger.

Tires are of prime importance to any cyclist. The need for strength and high quality is obvious, since a blowout on a motorcycle can cause a bad spill and perhaps serious injury. The tire tread must be chosen carefully. For trail riding, hill climbing, and other off-road activity, cross-grooved, lump-treaded tires, called "knobbies," are needed. They are designed to grip firmly on dirt and loose sand. But knobbies ride rough, wear quickly, and skid easily on pavement, therefore they should be used only for dirt riding.

For cycling under normal conditions, the more

28

conventional rib-treaded or diamond-patterned street tire has better traction, rides more smoothly, and is safer. The rib tread is not well suited to the dirt-gripping needs of off-pavement riding, or "cowtrailing," but, like motorcycles themselves, no tire fully fits all riding situations or purposes. Tire pressures should be checked carefully and maintained according to the manufacturer's recommendation. Either over inflating or under inflating is hazardous.

Handlebars should be strong, and cross-braced if necessary, for they take the brunt of most spills. They should be comfortable to the natural reach of the rider. The faddish towering, high-rise handlebars are fatiguing, inefficient, and impair visibility. In some areas they are illegal.

The best handlebars have a normal sweep that fits comfortably with the contour of the cycle and the rider's natural posture. The grips are low and bent to fit easily into the cyclist's hands, an essential accommodation, for assorted controls are attached to and near the grips. The handlebars should not have too wide a spread, or the tips may swing into the rider's body during a sharp turn. Wide handlebars also interfere with the motorcycle's ability to maneuver through narrow spaces.

Many motorcycles have a steering damper knob, usually located on the steering-head assembly. Tightening the knob stiffens the steering action, allowing the cycle to maintain a straight course with less effort and vibration when traveling over rough surfaces. For riding on smooth surfaces, the tension may be eased off.

In addition to a sturdy stand to support the cycle when it is not in use, strong horizontal pegs or footrests must be provided for both the driver and the passenger. If they are of the hinged variety so much the better. When not in use they can be folded up out of the way. The fewer objects protruding from a motorcycle the better. Foot pegs should be large enough to accommodate any foot or boot, and preferably rubber covered for firm gripping and comfort. They should be so placed to be within relaxed reach of the rider's feet when he is astride the vehicle. The passenger's pegs should be placed with equal care for comfort and safety.

Add a switch to get the whole thing started, and a horn to make his presence known, and the enthusiastic new cyclist has that two-wheeled vehicle upon which he can charge into new worlds of fun and adventure.

Of course, he first must learn to ride the machine!

LEARNING TO RIDE

A young person wouldn't think of driving the family car around the block without his learner's permit or driver's license tucked securely into his wallet. Only a very foolish person would attempt to fly an airplane without first undergoing a full course of pilot training to earn his pilot's license, or ticket.

Yet, in many parts of the country, at resorts, at fairs, or outdoor conventions, lightweight motorbikes are readily available to the completely inexperienced rider. In numerous towns and cities concessioners or overly eager cycle dealers for a few dollars will allow almost anybody to rent a motorcycle for an hour or so of fun that too often ends up with a mishap. Never-

32

theless, a person riding a cycle for the first time should be as carefully instructed as one starting to drive a car or fly a plane.

Most present-day traffic regulations apply equally to four- and two-wheeled motor vehicles. All prospective cycle riders should become thoroughly familiar with their local motor-vehicle code, copies of which are usually available at the nearest motor-vehicle department office. However, there is very little similarity in the actual operation of an automobile and a motorcycle, despite the fact that in many areas the same license enables a person to operate an automobile and a motorcycle.

Nor should a motorcycle be considered simply as a bicycle with a motor attached, and, therefore, easy to handle. Both motor scooters and motorcycles have distinctive handling characteristics, which must be mastered if a person hopes to ride with any degree of pleasure and safety. These driving techniques do not come naturally; they must be learned. Only after proper instruction can the beginner become a skilled, happy cyclist.

33

If he learns in hit-or-miss fashion—the hap-hazard "there's-the-throttle-there's-the-brake-take-her-for-a-spin" method—that same beginner becomes a prime candidate for the casualty list.

An increasing number of schools are offering motorcycle operator's training courses similar to the now well-established auto driver's training course. Often these programs are sponsored and conducted by local motorcycle dealers. Actually, learning to ride a motorcycle is not difficult. However, one still must be prepared properly to meet safely the varied challenges of cycling.

Training should begin from the moment a person approaches a dealer to look at a motorcycle. A reputable dealer will not simply point to a machine and tell the prospect what a good buy it is. He will spend some time asking questions concerning the uses the beginner intends to make of the machine. If, say, he wants it for transportation to school, general riding around town, plus maybe weekend fun riding the dirt trails outside the city limits, the salesman no doubt will steer him to a lightweight or middleweight bike suited

The buyer must examine every detail when selecting a cycle.

to both street touring and off-road exploring. Like a tailor, he will attempt to fit the machine to the customer.

Also, a reliable dealer will be concerned with the buyer's ability to ride. The dealer often offers

35

the beginner at no charge a full course of instructions on how to operate the cycle he buys. Police traffic departments and other interested agencies frequently provide free instructions in motorcycle riding. Sometimes the cycling student does not even need to own a machine. In fact, a few preliminary lessons may help him determine whether or not motorcycling is all he had imagined it to be, and how well it fits his needs and capabilities.

Learning to operate a motorcycle usually starts with becoming thoroughly familiar with the machine. The riding student walks around the cycle kicking the tires, as the saying goes. He studies it, noting as best he can which lever moves which control, what part is attached to what other part, and how they work together. He checks the condition of the cable leading from the squeeze lever on the right handlebar to the front brake. He notes which side the rear-brake pedal is on, and which side has the gearshift pedal, remembering that they vary with different makes of machines.

He twists the throttle on the right handlebar

grip. He feels whether it has a spring return so it will shut down automatically if released, a protection in case of a spill or loss of control. All throttles turn inward for added power, and outward, clockwise, to reduce or cut power. A common riding motto concerning the throttle is "When in doubt, turn *out!*"

The beginner keeps checking the machine and listening to the instructor explain each part and its function.

Now, with the cycle blocked up on its stand so the rear wheel is clear of the ground, the student climbs into the saddle. Before reaching for the switch, he makes a dry run through the controls. He tests the tension on the rear-brake pedal. He places his other boot on the foot peg so the heel rests against the rubber. He notes where the toe of his boot touches the gearshift pedal, both for pushing down and for toeing up.

The learner pays particular attention to the throttle on the right handlebar. He twists it several times to get the feel of it. He makes sure that the front-brake lever near the throttle is comfortably placed so he can squeeze it without having to remove his right hand from the throttle. The clutch lever on the left handlebar must be just as convenient and easy to operate.

With the machine still propped up on its stand or blocks, the novice rider checks to be sure the gearshift is in neutral position. Then he reaches beneath the gas tank and turns the gas petcock on. He turns on the ignition switch and sets the carburetor choke. He twists inward a little on the throttle to open the gas feed.

With his right foot on the kick starter, the cyclist gives it a firm and fast downward thrust, following through with whatever force is necessary to prevent compression recoil. The amount of strength needed on the kick starter depends largely upon the size of the engine. An increasing number of motorcycles now come equipped with electric starters, but the familiar kick starter is still most common.

Opposite: With the machine propped up on its stand the cyclist familiarizes himself with the controls.

Although the cyclist hopes the motorcycle will start with the first kick of the starter, perhaps several thrusts will be required to bring it to life. This hesitancy to start, incidentally, is an indication that the machine needs new sparkplugs and a tune-up.

Once the motor coughs into action, the student lets it idle for a half minute or so, warming it up slowly to avoid motor damage often caused by gunning a cold engine. Also a cold engine is prone to missing or stalling. After the proper warm-up the cyclist releases the choke.

He is now ready to go—except, due to being up on the stand or blocks, the cycle's rear wheel is still off the ground. That's fine. While he straddles a live engine, the beginner simulates an actual ride. He runs through the gears, squeezing the clutch lever between each shift. He coordinates the throttle to each change of gears. He closes the throttle quickly during the shifting, then immediately feeds gas to maintain speed. The jacked-up rear wheel spins, going nowhere. Gaining familiarity with the machine, the new cyclist tries his brakes, both front and rear, to get the feel of them. He even practices shifting down into lower gears, using engine compression to help slow him down and take some of the strain off the brakes.

He practices under his instructor's critical eyes. Thus, the new rider establishes proper motorcycling habits from the very beginning.

Then, and not until then, is it time to get the cycle off its stand and onto the road. The instructor can tell when his student is ready. Actually, riding a motorcycle is scarcely more difficult than riding a bicycle (some claim it's easier), but there is power to harness and extra controls to master. The consequences of shabby operation can prove much more serious than is normally encountered in bicycling.

To start out, the new rider picks a vacant parking lot, a smooth field, or a quiet, isolated stretch of neighborhood street. There he can practice riding without the added worry of traffic. Perhaps at first he rides tandem with his instructor sitting behind him, reaching around and handling some of the controls. The beginner watches and listens, observing the sequence in which the instructor moves the controls and the ease with which he does it. Or perhaps the instructor trots along beside the machine for a way, watching, while the new rider stays in low gear, using little throttle, and going just fast enough to maintain good balance.

Finally the time comes for the student to take the machine out alone. With his left hand he squeezes the clutch lever just before moving the gearshift lever with his foot. He lets out the clutch. The cycle moves forward. If he coordinates his movements, he will accelerate smoothly. If his movements have been clumsy, the cycle will jerk forward, and the nervous beginner probably will kill the engine. He should avoid looking at the controls, operating them by feel alone. His attention must be concentrated on the road ahead.

As essential as being able to move forward easily is being able to stop both smoothly and quickly. This operation requires more care and skill than stopping an automobile. There is good reason for having separate controls for both front and rear brakes of a motorcycle. The rear brake operated by the foot pedal is most important, and generally it is used first. Applied correctly, it slows down the cycle without putting it into a skid. Applied too hard at excessive speed, it will throw the motorcycle into a sure skid. This maneuver may well "lay it down" on its side, usually damaging both rider and machine.

Learning to use the brake controls correctly takes considerable practice. Motorcycle tires have a small area of friction or adhesion to a road surface. Consequently skids are quite easily induced. Using the rear brake properly tends to keep the machine on a straight course while it slows down. Usually the stopping power of the front brake should be added, although in a manner gentle enough not to cause the rear end to skid or fishtail around. Applying the front brake alone, particularly if the cycle is in a turn, or the wheel is cocked, can cause severe tumbles.

With practice, the new rider learns to coor-

43

dinate the two brakes in order to maintain proper balance. He may learn in time to rely more on the front brake than on the rear. All braking should be as soft and unhurried as is practical in the situation. In any event, if the cyclist finds himself having to put the motorcycle into a skidding stop, chances are he has been going too fast for safety.

In fact, as experience increases, the motorcycle rider will seldom use his brakes at all. Instead, he will downshift into lower gears and use engine compression to slow the vehicle.

Having become thoroughly familiar with his cycle—clutch, gearshift, throttle, brakes—the rider is ready to head cautiously for the open road. At moderate speeds he learns what a sensitive machine he straddles. It will accelerate like a greyhound. When starting out, unless the cyclist is gentle with the throttle, he may end up doing a "wheelie," a maneuver in which the front wheel rears up from the ground. It may even throw him into a backward somersault.

The cyclist learns, too, that the spinning wheels

44

of a moving motorcycle have a gyroscopic effect on the machine. Anyone who has rolled an old automobile tire down a path, running beside it and coaxing it along with slaps from his hand, knows how the gyroscopic effect, or centrifugal force, of a spinning object works. As long as it keeps rolling, the tire remains upright. But if it is brought to a very slow speed or stopped entirely, the tire will topple over. This same gyroscopic force generated by its turning wheels helps keep a motorcycle balanced upright. Also, the moving cycle is inclined to maintain a straight course until pressure is exerted to change its direction. To exert this pressure and turn the cycle, the rider needs merely to lean a bit, shifting his weight in the desired direction. The motorcycle naturally follows through. Most of the time the cyclist doesn't even turn the handlebars. He just leans.

But he mustn't lean too far, for gravity, too, plays a part in cycle riding. Gravity wants to tip the cycle onto its lowest surface, which is its side. Thus, balance must be maintained constantly.

45

In Los Angeles recently, the police department, a large automobile club, and an interested motorcycle dealer who provided the machines, set up a pilot program to train members of an Explorer Scout Post who were interested in learning to motorcycle. The program was divided into four phases.

The fourteen boys first spent thirty-two hours on classroom work, meeting on Saturday mornings in a local church youth hall. There they learned the basic rules of safe driving, reviewed traffic laws, and discussed the techniques of *defensive driving*. Defensive driving means that the motorcyclist—or automobile driver, for that matter—must keep constantly alert to possible emergencies building up around him. He must be in full control of his machine at all times. He must keep his speed down and keep a comfortable distance between himself and any possible hazard. This observance allows him ample time to take defensive, evasive action should danger occur.

Phase two of the Explorer Scout training pro-

The Explorers practice motorcycle control
over a pylon-marked course.

gram took them outside the classroom to get acquainted with the motorcycle itself. The instructor
described the controls and demonstrated their
functions. Next the Explorers were given actual
riding lessons on a vacant parking lot. Under
close supervision they were allowed to practice
riding along pylon-marked routes. Then, still
closely supervised, the young riders were allowed

to take the machines out onto quiet public streets.

By this time each boy was well acquainted with his cycle, its capabilities and limitations. Each boy rode with growing confidence.

For the final gala event of the training program, the class took a two-hundred mile overnight round-trip tour into the San Bernardino Mountains. They were convoyed by off-duty policemen and other volunteers interested in young people and in correct, safe motorcycling.

Not a single accident of any kind marred this carefully planned and skillfully executed training program. As numbers of two-wheeled vehicles continue to increase, similar types of training programs will be made available to interested young riders. These programs will be a giant step toward proper motorcycling.

Once having mastered the techniques of motorcycle riding, a person is ready to join the ranks of veterans. How long he will remain a member in good standing will be in almost direct proportion to how carefully and diligently he abides by the rules of cycling safety.

48

SAFETY FIRST!

The most important factor and greatest need in all motorcycling is safety.

Riding out in the open as he does, the cyclist is exposed to injury in case of any serious skid or collision. Therefore, it is important that he dress as protectively as possible. Of utmost necessity is the wearing of a properly fitted and reinforced helmet. The vast majority of serious cycle injuries and deaths involve the head. A cheap helmet is of little value. A proper helmet is one approved by some such testing firm as the American Standards Association or accepted by the American Motorcycle Association (AMA).

There are numerous helmet designs. Those styled after football or jet-pilot helmets give full head and ear protection. For maximum safety they seem the best. Covering the ears, however, hinders hearing. Other helmets are designed more like workers' hardhats; they have fabric or leather chin straps, which also protect the ears and do not shut out sound as much. The main requirements of any helmet are that it cover and protect a maximum area of the head, that it be well constructed, and that it be properly padded.

The helmet should be light colored, preferably white, to reflect the sun's heat, as well as to be more visible both day and night. Some helmets are finished with reflectorizing paint, which glows at night when caught in any beam of light. Similar reflecting paint or strips may be added to the motorcycle itself for night safety. Certainly the helmet can be decorated to suit the fancy of its wearer. But it should always be worn, and worn proudly. It is the mark of an experienced motorcyclist who places a value on his life.

Opposite: A well-constructed, padded helmet, preferably white, should be worn while cycling.

The motorcyclist should wear as much other protective clothing as the weather will permit. Long sleeves and heavy jackets, preferably leather, minimize abrasions should the cycle flip. Strips of reflective material sewn to a jacket also help night drivers see the cyclist.

Gloves and high shoes or boots are recommended for additional safety and comfort. Goggles are important to protect the rider's eyes from wind and debris. Usually two pairs of goggles are needed—a tinted pair for daytime and a clear pair for nighttime.

When riding, the motorcyclist must be careful to observe rules of safety. Actually he has more to think about than the motorist and must be a better driver than the passenger-car operator. For one thing, he is more vulnerable than the motorist who is surrounded by protective steel.

To survive in such an uneven match, the wise motorcyclist drives defensively at all times. In fact, the cyclist should drive as though all automobiles and trucks are after him. This attitude will keep him alert to the driver who turns left without signaling, swings into a driveway from the wrong lane, or makes some other unexpected move. Whether the motorist is right or wrong is of small concern to the injured cyclist if an accident should occur.

Consequently, the good cyclist thinks ahead. He can't afford to daydream or let his mind wander. He must see the chuckhole in front of him. He must be careful when approaching railroad tracks set in the street and maneuver his cycle to cross them head on. If he attempts to cross at too parallel an angle, or tries riding along the tracks, his narrow cycle tires may catch in the ruts and flip him.

He must watch for the buildup of any accident-producing situation. A wet road, a grease spot on a corner, a car approaching an intersection or backing out of a driveway, a canine "tirebiter" in yapping pursuit—these and an infinite number of other conditions signal a possible accident in the making.

The cyclist must assume that the motorist doesn't see him and must constantly protect his

53

margin of safety. Most automobiles have numerous blind spots, and their drivers are inclined to be on the lookout for larger hazards. Consequently, auto drivers often see right through, past, or over the motorcycle.

Even more than the four-wheeled motorist, the motorcyclist must know and abide by the various rules and courtesies of the road. His mistakes and oversights can be more costly. A cyclist with automobile-driving experience will have an idea of how a motorist thinks and acts. Also he will have learned something about the basic mechanics of motion—starting, stopping, changing direction—which apply to all vehicles.

By thinking ahead and driving defensively
a cyclist will avoid such close calls as this one.

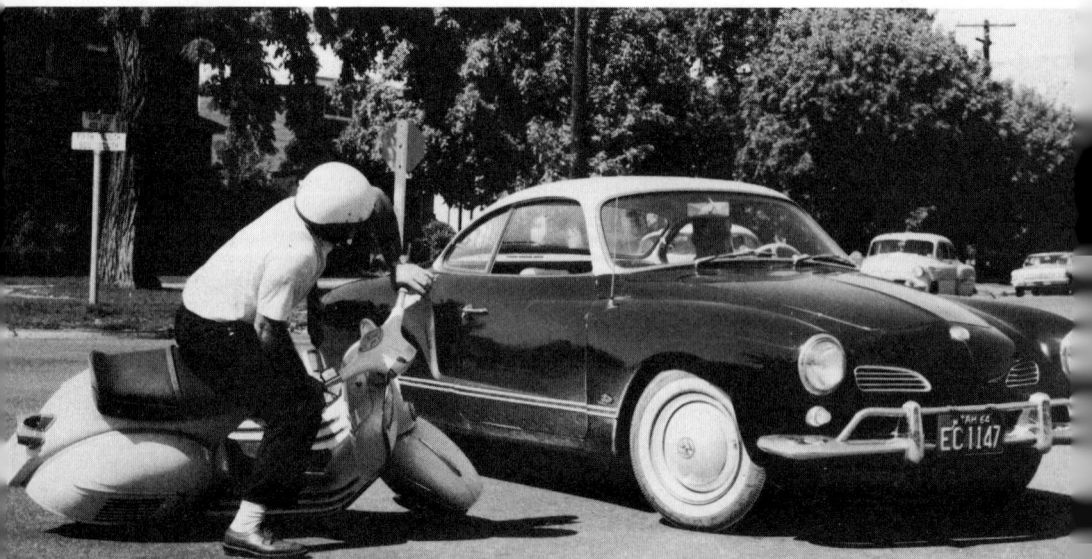

By driving defensively the motorcyclist is constantly on the alert for the sudden red flash of a stoplight on the third or fourth car up ahead. Thus, at the first flicker, he can touch his own brake or otherwise prepare to avoid piling into the buildup of hard-braking cars.

When driving along a high-speed road, the cyclist should maintain his position in the center or left center of the lane. Thus he occupies his rightful road space completely and prevents a motorist from pulling up beside him and crowding him off to the right of the lane. The cyclist must position himself far enough back and to the left so he can see beyond the car in front of him. If he follows directly behind the car, he loses visibility of the road ahead. He invites disaster by hitting a bump or other obstruction that the automobile blots from vision.

Tailgating on a motorcycle is potentially more disastrous than in a car. Any sudden stop leaves the cyclist little alternative but to crash into the car's rear end.

Among the many objects that are potential

hazards to the motorcyclist are holes in the road surface and concrete channels used to drain off water at intersections. They can flip a motorcycle as quickly as railroad tracks can. Then there are always bottles, cans, sticks, stones, and other debris to watch out for. Objects such as hubcaps or muffler parts are forever falling off cars to become waiting snares for the unwary cyclist. Cats, dogs, and even birds become hazards to the cyclist whose balance is easily disrupted.

Unsafe road conditions are created by oil, water, mud, ice, wet leaves, sand, gravel, and numerous other skid-inducing substances. The wise motorcyclist pays constant attention to his riding. Knowing that the equilibrium of a motorcycle can be upset easily, the experienced rider shuns any unfamiliar road condition since it may prove troublesome. Even the somewhat slippery white-painted lines separating the highway lanes can be risky.

A cyclist must always keep his speed down sufficiently to be able to come to a quick stop in time to avoid contact. Hand signals should be

56

used by cyclists just as they are by motorists—
hand down for slow or stop, left hand straight out
for a left turn, up for a right turn. As an additional precaution, the cyclist should always check
his mirror and glance back over his shoulder before making his turn to determine that the way
is clear. He should do his braking before reaching the turn, not while he is in it.

The cyclist needs to be as aware of pedestrians
as is the motorist. He must watch for children
darting out from between cars, for shoppers in
crosswalks, and for any other people who may
not hear or see him in time to avoid an entangle-
ment. Even people who are inclined to keep a
cautious lookout for automobiles seldom consider
the possibility of being run down by a motorcycle. It can and does happen, with discomfort or
injury to both parties.

Since motorcycles are not easily seen, the
headlight and taillight should be used freely. It is
a good habit to turn them on an hour or so before
other vehicles do, and many cyclists believe in
leaving their motorcycle lights on all the time

they are riding. If widely accepted, this practice may well diminish many of the accidents that occur simply because the cycle was not seen by the other party. Of course, one should drive even more slowly at night than during the day.

The cyclist who zooms between cars, often along the white divider lines, is riding for a quick fall. To have a car squeeze in on him unknowingly is a shortcut to disaster. When passing an automobile, the cyclist should allow plenty of room, pass always on the left, signal properly, and get back into his lane as quickly as possible.

When the cyclist drives defensively, he keeps one eye on the driver in the car ahead. He watches for any slight movement of head or arms that may indicate the driver is about to turn or stop. Meanwhile, through the rear-view mirrors attached to his handlebars, the motorcyclist keeps alert to what is happening behind him.

Mention should be made of motorcycle noise. Loud, raucous muffler—or mufflerless—sound is one of the major detractors from the good image of motorcycling. Motorcycles without mufflers have no place on public streets and highways, and in many areas they are outlawed. Most types of street and touring motorcycles come equipped with effective mufflers, which dampen the noise down to a comfortable and acceptable level. To tamper with the muffler in any way not only defeats its purpose of abating the sound, but upsets the balance of engine power. In addition to being a public nuisance, a loud motorcycle sprinting past an automobile can so startle the driver as to cause an accident, in which case the cyclist may become even more dangerously involved.

There are a few simple safety hints that too often are learned the hard way. A motorcycle has a fairly high center of gravity, particularly with a rider in the saddle. The engine is set as low in the frame as possible to keep the machine from being overly top-heavy, particularly at slow speed where the balancing gyroscopic force of the spinning wheels tends to lessen. One should be careful of adding more weight at a high level. Carrying packages in the arms or on the handlebars can easily cause loss of control. Packages should

59

be secured to a rack. They should not be piled high, where they may upset balance and are susceptible to crosswinds.

The carrying of passengers should be left to the expert riders, or at least put off until a rider has had ample cycling experience. With a passenger on the back of the cycle, the problem of control is much more critical. Too often passengers lean in an attempt to balance the machine, causing the unprepared driver real problems. If a passenger is to ride on the buddy seat, he must first be given proper instructions by the driver. He should grip the handholds provided or grasp the driver's waist. Above all, the passenger should let the driver do the leaning and shifting of weight that is necessary to any maneuver.

Courtesy of the road is part of safety. The motorcyclist must think of the other person, regardless of who really has the right-of-way. It is easy to notice the courtesy, or the lack of it, on the part of a cyclist who sits out in the open on his two-wheeler. He is always under the critical eye

Carrying a passenger requires skill
and full attention to the rules of safety.

of a passenger-car driver, who may not himself
be courteous, but expects it from his lightweight
and often noisy competitor. A bit of politeness

may cause motorists to be more sympathetic to cyclists and concerned with their safety.

Actually, although much justifiable stress is put upon safety factors in motorcycling, calmness, caution, and common sense will ensure safety in most situations.

The rewards for such safe practices will be the endless fun and freedom of the road for the motorcyclist.

PLEASURE RIDING

Today literally millions of people daily take to both highways and byways on the two-wheelers. Some use motorcycles simply for necessary transportation as one might use the less economical and less maneuverable automobile. Others head for the open spaces on pleasure or camping trips. Still others disdain pavement and set out on off-road explorations into the backcountry.

The largest motorcycle tour in the world takes place each fall when thousands of motorcyclists ride across the plains, pour through mountain canyons, and cross desert wastes to meet for a weekend of fun and friendship in Death Valley, California. They arrive from all directions and from nearly every state in the country. With some

63

3,000 or more cyclists participating, the weekend is one of unique two-wheeled activity. Various riding and non-riding contests include such events as touring the scenic desert wasteland and frying flapjacks.

No one takes the program too seriously, but everyone enjoys the companionship of other cyclists and the chance to show off his immaculately groomed machine. Friendships are made and renewed year after year at the meeting on the moonlike landscape of Death Valley. In less spectacular settings throughout the nation many similar get-togethers are held by socially minded motorcycle-touring riders, who use their machines at least partly for fresh-air enjoyment.

Literally thousands of two-wheeled riding groups and motorcycle clubs have developed in the United States. Some are organized and follow a calendar of planned events throughout the year. Others are informal, perhaps neighborhood groups of young people who band together to share cycling fun and adventure.

Local motorcycle dealers usually can guide a

new cyclist to a group that closely fits his type of machine, his capabilities, and his riding interests. A touring or camping group often is made up of riders who own the middleweight or big bikes. They need something large enough to carry food, clothing, and traveling equipment. The larger cycles also are comfortable enough to ride for longer distances. Such clubs often can be identified by their distinctly colored blazers or jackets, which sport their private insignia.

Trail or off-road riding is extremely popular

Riding clubs enable members to share all the fun of cycling.

with cyclists of all ages. There is no minimum age involved, and no license needed, since public thoroughfares are not used. The restrictions of common sense and safety, of course, must be observed.

An off-road club, often made up of family groups, will tend toward the lighter-weight machines. An off-road cycle usually is stripped down for trail and dirt riding and is equipped with knobby tires for traction in the dirt. Such a machine has little use for lights, and full front and rear fenders are often more hindrance than help. A trail machine will have a steel guard plate beneath the motor to protect it from damage by rocks, logs, or other back-country materials. Also perhaps a brush bar will be mounted behind the front wheel to keep branches and trail debris from punishing the engine and the cyclist's legs. Usually the mufflers are mounted high and out of the way of trail hazards. It is a good idea for the cyclist to carry on trail trips at least a small tool kit, plus an extra master link or two for the drive chain.

66

Many of the most popular, inexpensive, off-road machines are too low powered and low geared to be able to keep up with the normal flow of highway traffic, and therefore must stay off high-speed thoroughfares. Usually such bikes are

Off-road cycles feature knobby tires
and are usually stripped down.

Handy bumper racks can haul trail bikes to dirt country.

carried by car to the scene of the dirt-trail action.
Even though ruled off turnpikes and freeways,
the low-powered, low-geared machines usually
are suitable for simple neighborhood or school
transportation chores. Sometimes they are
adapted to street riding by using an alternate rear
chain sprocket, which increases the cycle's speed.

The off-road riding machines often substitute a
rear rack for the buddy seat. The rear rack is

68

handy for carrying whatever fuel, food, or gear may be needed for fun in the backcountry. Some of the lightweights will faithfully carry a rider and a couple of hundred pounds of gear over the roughest kind of wooded, mountainous, or desert country.

Dirt riding is exciting and great fun; however, it requires both skill and responsibility. Except in extremely rough terrain, or at a very slow speed, the rider should keep his feet on the pegs. He should resort to footing—aiding balance by dropping one or both feet to the ground—only when necessary to maintain full control over the machine.

The trail rider often encounters gullies, ravines, hills, and sand. He must be a master of his transmission. He must know which gear is suited to each uphill, downhill, mud, or sand situation. He must know how to use both brakes, plus low-gear engine compression to maintain control while dropping down over a sheer hillside. Experience will show that on most steep downgrades applying the brakes in a series of short on-off-on-off movements controls the machine better than jamming them on and holding them.

If he stalls on a steep uphill trail, the wise rider will usually squeeze the front brake hard and dismount on the uphill side so the machine won't fall on him. He keeps a firm hold on the handlebars. Then he can wrestle the machine around to a position in which he can restart it. Or he can turn it around and coast back downhill.

Over extremely rough or steep terrain a motorcyclist will sometimes dismount and "walk" the machine across or up the barrier while it is running in low gear. If his route becomes too rough, or too steep, the cyclist can simply lay the machine on its side while he figures out his next move.

Certainly the joys of trail riding are as wide and varied as the fields and forests, mountains, deserts, and seashores. The fisherman and hunter can get into areas once accessible only to pack-

Opposite: The trail-riding motorcyclist must have completely mastered the control of his machine.

horses. Since remoteness is one of the pleasant parts of trail riding, the cyclist should always ride with at least one companion. Then in case of a personal mishap or mechanical trouble, there is someone to lend a hand or go for help.

Trail riding puts much responsibility upon the cyclist. If either written or unwritten rules and courtesies are ignored, the motorcyclist can quickly lose his freedom of movement. He should never cross private property without first obtain-

"Cowtrailing" into the backcountry
is part of the fun of motorcycling.

ing permission from the owner. If permission is granted, he should do all in his power to be considerate of the privilege by not disrupting land or livestock. He should leave gates as he finds them, either open or closed, and should keep down noise by using an approved muffler.

National parks and forests welcome cyclists who abide by the simple rules of common sense and courtesy. All riding must be along established trails. Attempting to cut new trails or taking shortcuts breaks down slopes, causes soil damage, and otherwise opens up the ground to erosion. Speed should be held down to ensure the safety of not only the rider, but the hiker or horseman who may be just around the bend. Courteous cyclists will stop and turn off their motors until the horses have passed.

All other rules of forests or parks should be observed. And in forest or dry grass country, the motorcycle must be equipped with a spark arrester on the muffler. When trail riding in a national forest or park, the cyclist should check in with the ranger and provide at least a tentative

73

schedule of his activity. Then the ranger knows where to begin to look for the rider in case he doesn't return as planned. Also the ranger, knowing the trail conditions, will specify open and closed areas. He can furnish fire permits, maps, and pertinent information. He may also remind the cyclist that designated primitive areas, fire danger zones, and other posted lands are closed to *all* motorized vehicles, including motorcycles.

The variety of both street-riding activity and off-road adventures is as widespread as the motorcyclist's imagination, providing him with fresh air, freedom of movement, and invigorating challenge.

THE WORKING
TWO-WHEELERS

Motorcycles have proved extremely useful for many work requirements. Probably their most familiar use is in police work. For decades traffic enforcement officers have found that their capacity for quick acceleration, high-speed running, and easy maneuverability make motorcycles very handy instruments for catching and apprehending traffic violators and other law breakers. Policemen use the heavy machines, complete with red lights, sirens, and two-way radios.

Easy mobility often enables motorcycle officers to reach a scene of emergency well ahead of others. A few years ago during the disastrous Bel Air fire near Los Angeles, motorcycle officers Greg Atcheson and Hugh Murchison, Jr. heard

75

the police broadcast the SOS over their radios.

As they raced up the tinder-dry canyon toward a group of houses in the path of the fast-moving blaze, the men saw the panicked people fleeing frantically from the approaching fire, carrying whatever personal belongings they could.

The narrow road was quickly clogged with stalled cars. But the two officers were able to weave their cycles through the congestion toward the homes that appeared doomed to the racing flames. Then, unbelievably, the officers spotted

Motorcycle officers rescue children from a roaring inferno.

a pair of wild-eyed children isolated by the blaze behind a house. Officers Atcheson and Murchison charged through the smoke and rain of hot fire-brands, scooped up the two- and three-year-old youngsters, hauled them to safety, then returned to guide other people away from the fire.

Similar on-the-spot rescue operations during fire, flood, or other catastrophes fall regularly into the motorcycle officer's tour of duty. They often for this reason draw extra pay. To be competent for such tasks motorcycle officers undergo

Motorcycle police in training practice rough off-road riding.

a rigorous course of training. Recruits for motor-cycle patrol duty often emerge from the ranks of young hobby riders or cowtrailing enthusiasts. However, most any well-coordinated, intelligent, and alert young man whose interests lie in law enforcement and public welfare stands a good chance of being accepted for police training.

In recent years motorcycles and helicopters have teamed up for traffic control as well as law enforcement. A truck-trailer turns over, blocking a turnpike or freeway and threatening to trigger a series of rear-end crashes. The chopper cruising overhead spots the accident and traffic snarl. Immediately it reports the situation by radio to the motorcycle officers below. The cyclists maneuver their small machines through the growing pack of jammed vehicles. Arriving at the hub of the tieup, they take over and redirect traffic to get it moving again as quickly as possible.

All in all, the motorcycle officers of the country form a ready mobile force available for any type of civic function from leading a parade to controlling a riot.

Throughout the country three-wheeler motorcycles are used by police departments for marking or ticketing cars parked overtime. Many other three-wheelers are used by the post office for delivering mail and packages. Two-wheeled cycles, maneuverable in traffic, are essential for the rapid delivery of small items such as prescriptions. Movie films often are shuttled from one theater to another by motorcycle courier.

Many craftsmen, salesmen, and businessmen use motorcycles for traveling back and forth to their work in offices, factories, and other business establishments. Economy and ease of parking are dividends along with the healthful joy of fresh-air activity.

The motorcycle is, all in all, a versatile machine. In an age of growing congestion—when getting from one place to another often presents a complicated problem—motorcycles are being discovered as something of a magic carpet, short-cutting across both time and space.

It is no mystery why the motorcycle has become the symbol of the action generation.

TWO-WHEELED SPORT

Sooner or later nearly every motorcyclist yearns to pit his riding skills against those of others. Although there are a few professional motorcycle racers, just as there are professional racing-car drivers, the overwhelming majority of cycle riders retain their amateur standing. They race around dirt ovals, climb precarious hillsides, slog through swamps or woodlands, and battle the clock for the sheer joy and excitement of competition.

Two or more people on motorcycles can measure their riding skills against each other in many informal ways. The contest can be anything from a simple treasure hunt to a soccer game on lightweight machines or an impromptu race along a

80

vacant stretch of beach that ends up as a free-for-all struggle to reach the top of a distant hill.

As in any type of motorcycle riding, the prime considerations in competition are riding experience and attention to safety factors. Much of this competition is spontaneous and unorganized. However, cyclists who have tasted the heady delights of neighborhood victories and wish to take part in more highly organized contests can consider joining the American Motorcycle Association (AMA) or other organizations for cycles.

The AMA encourages formation of motorcycling clubs and sanctions some 4,000 different competitive amateur and professional meets a year. Only members of the AMA are allowed to enter these contests so sponsors and contestants are reasonably sure that each rider has experience, practices proper safety, and will not become a hazard in competition. The AMA has headquarters in Worthington, Ohio, and local district representatives govern activities within their own areas. All groups adhere to basic AMA rules and by-laws.

A motorcyclist who competes in AMA-sanc-
tioned events in which prize money is paid loses
amateur standing, and he must carry a competition license indicating his professional status.
Most cycling competition, however, is composed
of amateur events in which, at most, a trophy
may be offered.

As in most any other sport, there is a small
group of trained professional motorcycle riders

Winning the Daytona 200 is a heady victory for any cyclist.

who manage to make a living by barnstorming around the country entering different motorcycling events. Many of them operate dealerships or motorcycle shops during the off-season, and a few lucky ones are sponsored by cycle manufacturers.

As important as the prize money these professionals collect is the pursuit of the national championship of motorcycling. National championships are based on an accumulation of points earned in a variety of nationwide events. The current national champion has the privilege of sporting a number 1 on his cycle.

A wide assortment of competitive motorcycling events take place in this country. Each requires varying degrees of skill and stamina. Only by scouting around and trying a few of them out can the eager new rider determine which best suits his abilities and interests. Plenty of riders have a great deal of fun, while at the same time improving their cycling skills, by entering informally organized field meets. These competitions may take place on vacant lots, in parks, or on some field on the outskirts of town. Success depends largely upon the enthusiasm of the cyclists and on there being enough spirited members of the group with a knack for thinking up a series of events challenging to perform on a motorcycle.

A field meet is a funfest, a collection of games on two wheels, with hazards kept at a minimum. One common event is a Slow Race. Here contestants race the clock backwards, taking as much time as possible to ride between two points without losing balance and having to "dab" a foot (touch the ground), leave the course path, or kill the engine. There's a Boot Race in which all contestants' boots are tossed in a pile. En route to victory, the riders must find and don their own boots. Naturally, in the search, loose boots get thrown wildly in all directions.

Then there are contests in which riders try to "build" a hot dog, mustard and all, without stopping their machines, a difficult feat, since one hand is always needed on the throttle. There are barrel-rolling contests and any number of other stunts to perform while chugging along on a

84

cycle. Such field meets are like picnics or Sunday outings. They really need no sanction or sponsorship other than a bunch of cheerful cyclists out for a good time and off-road fun. As a by-product of the horseplay, however, beginning cyclists gain valuable experience. Of course, such cycling games are illegal on public thoroughfares.

As a rider becomes more proficient on his machine, he may enter more advanced events. The popular English trials is a danger-free race in which riders traverse rough terrain on a course that has been marked out in tape. Similar to a miniature golf course, a trials course may cover very little ground, but have obstacles such as sand traps, water hazards, steep slopes, gullies, sharp curves, and so forth. Speed is no great factor, but control of the machine is. The rider loses points for dabbing a foot to the ground, crossing taped course lines, stopping, stalling the engine, or showing any other indications of poor control over his vehicle.

Having acquired full confidence and mastered his motorcycle, the amateur rider may progress

85

to the road run, an event like a sports-car rally, except it is for two-wheeled vehicles instead of four-wheeled ones. A road run is both a race and an exercise in navigation. Routes are established, checkpoints set up, and each contestant must follow clues in order to be first to reach his destination and the winner's circle.

While the race is going on, the cyclist also may find himself cruising through some scenic country. The road run, like straight touring for pleasure, is on prepared surfaces, including both paved highways and gravel or graded back roads. It is easy on machines and riders, and much preferred by many cyclists who don't relish such backbreaking, tire-pounding events as scrambles or enduros.

A scramble is a race conducted over a closed-circuit, dirt-track obstacle course. Here the rider must contend with sand, jumps, twists, turns, and assorted other riding hazards. There is no standard course for scrambles. As long as the route is difficult to maneuver around, it will suffice.

Actually, Grand Prix motorcycle racing—

86

which requires a high degree of skill—is a form of scrambling, but over longer and more rugged courses.

An endurance race, called an "enduro," is a clocked event over an unfamiliar course having a full share of woods, desert, or other rough terrain. Contests usually run for two days or so,

An enduro race is usually a grueling, dirt-digging, mud-slogging event.

cover upwards of 300 rugged miles, and really test the staying power of both man and machine. The rider does not try to beat the clock, but to ride on a fixed schedule and hit each checkpoint on the split second if possible. Being too fast costs points as well as being too slow.

One of the favorite endurance races is the hare-and-hounds. Dozens of cycles usually participate in this grueling event. Any cross-country course that includes little-used roads, dirt trails, hilly and difficult terrain can become the scene of a hare-and-hounds event.

Prior to the race, the long course is established by the hare, who marks the route with sporadic splashes of lime. The riders—the hounds—must hit assorted checkpoints during the pursuit. Other than that requirement, the race is to the swift. Some hare-and-hound races include a class for motorcycles with sidecars. That, indeed, is a rough way to travel!

A racing event of great magnitude is the hare-and-hounds race which takes place periodically on California's Mojave Desert. As the sun rises, casting long shadows from gnarled Joshua trees, spiny cactus, and scrub brush of all kinds, hundreds of contestants kick their two-wheelers to life and roar off across the sandy, rock-strewn desert.

Before the day is over, many contestants have dropped by the wayside from sheer fatigue or their cycles have been put out of working order by fouled sparkplugs, flat tires, broken chains, or any of numerous other mischances that may befall a cyclist along the scorching (up to 130 degrees) course. Fortunately, due to frequent checkpoints and constant patrolling, by the end of the day all riders are accounted for. The broken-down machines are wrestled out of prickly barricades of underbrush or wallows of deep sand. A tired, grimy, but happy winner is declared.

Days later riders are still nursing bruises, scratches, and sore muscles, while busily repairing abused machines. The Mojave Desert hare-and-hounds is a race that no one in his right mind would try a second time. Yet, most riders who have done it once can't wait to tackle it again.

Many variations exist in scrambles, enduros, cross-country, hare-and-hounds, and Grand Prix motorcycle racing. All the races, however, call upon a full measure of endurance from both men and machines.

Other riders prefer motorcycle hill climbing. In this timed event the cyclists begin at a starting line at the bottom and ride to the top of a steep dirt hill. Although the event produces a fair share of spills, few serious accidents occur because the cycle's motor is rigged to cut off automatically when there's an upset. For the occasional cyclist who uses his vehicle mostly for transportation to school or for simple everyday riding, hill climbing is a better sport to watch than to enter. Hill-climbing cycles usually are stripped-down models that will not be damaged easily. Still, moderate hills attract all riders, and rare is the two-wheeler who has not tried his hand at the slopes.

Drag racing on motorcycles is almost as popu-

Opposite: During a hill-climbing event a competitor frequently has only one wheel on the ground.

90

lar as the four-wheeled drags. The cycles use the same quarter-mile strip, burn lots of rubber leaving the starting gate, and can hit fantastic speeds of around 150 miles per hour in the ten seconds sometimes needed to cover the distance. These drag-racing cycles are invariably custom built. They are fueled with special exotic mixes and use oversize rear tires, which furnish the essential traction for the blast-off and sprint. Drag races may be either time trials or races between individual contestants, and the various divisions are organized by type of cycle and size of engine.

Some communities conduct open competition for standard cycles ridden by sufficiently qualified and experienced cyclists. In any case, drag racing has its full share of dangers. It should never be attempted on neighborhood streets or, for that matter, anywhere except on an approved strip, and only under proper supervision.

For the ultimate in two-wheeled speed, each August motorcyclists in specially built machines head for the vast, smooth salt flats of Bonneville, Utah, where all world land speed records have been set. There, huddled inside streamlined, cigar-shaped wind farings, drivers of two-wheelers, which hardly resemble motorcycles at all, have exceeded speeds of 255 miles per hour. At this time, speed cyclists are striving for 300 miles per hour. That, indeed, is a motorcycling event in which few participate.

Also limited to a special group of cyclists is the track racing on dirt or boards that one sees

Specially built two-wheelers regularly break world speed records on Bonneville salt flats.

on television or at country fairs. This racing is strictly a spectator sport, except for the small handful of professional cyclists who broadside around the curves with an iron-shod left shoe scraping the dirt for balance and stability. The cycles used in such races are without brakes, and the contestants usually wear long-sleeved leather clothing, called simply leathers, to offer them some protection in the event of a high-speed spill. Perhaps not strictly for professionals, this type of racing does require professional skills.

All in all, whether the competition is organized, or merely confined to a few eager enthusiasts anxious to pit their riding skills against each other, cycling for sport accounts for a large percentage of all motorcycling.

But no matter for what type of work, sport, or simple pleasure the cyclist uses his machine, his success and enjoyment will depend on the practiced skill and concern for safety with which he rides his vehicle. Motorcycling is a two-wheeled world opening ever wider to exploration by the adventurous young.

94

INDEX

*indicates illustrations